Author:

Anne Rooney studied English at Cambridge University, England, and then earned a Ph.D. at Cambridge. She has held teaching posts at several UK universities and is currently a Royal Literary Fund fellow at Newnham College, Cambridge. She has written more than 150 books for children and adults, including several on the history of science and medicine. She also writes children's fiction.

Artist:

Mark Bergin was born in Hastings, England, in 1961. He studied at Eastbourne College of Art and specializes in historical reconstructions, aviation, and maritime subjects. He lives in Bexhill-on-Sea with his wife and children.

Series creator:

David Salariya was born in Dundee, Scotland. He has illustrated a wide range of books and has created and designed many new series for publishers in the UK and overseas. David established The Salariya Book Company in 1989. He lives in Brighton, England, with his wife, illustrator Shirley Willis, and their son, Jonathan.

Editor: **Jacqueline Ford**

Editorial Assistant: **Mark Williams**

PAPER FROM
SUSTAINABLE
FORESTS

Published in Great Britain in 2017 by
The Salariya Book Company Ltd
25 Marlborough Place, Brighton BN1 1UB

ISBN-13: 978-0-531-22461-8 (lib. bdg.) 978-0-531-22490-8 (pbk.)

All rights reserved.
Published in 2017 in the United States
by Franklin Watts
An imprint of Scholastic Inc.

A CIP catalog record for this book is available
from the Library of Congress.

Printed and bound in China.
Printed on paper from sustainable sources.
1 2 3 4 5 6 7 8 9 10 R 26 25 24 23 22 21 20 19 18 17

SPEED LIMIT 45

You Wouldn't Want to Live Without™
Math!

Written by
Anne Rooney

Illustrated by
Mark Bergin

Series created by
David Salariya

Franklin Watts®
An Imprint of Scholastic Inc.

Contents

Introduction

How much do you like math? Maybe you enjoy number games? You might not like numbers as much when you have to do your math homework, but it would be really hard to live without them. You wouldn't just miss out on puzzles and games.

Imagine how difficult life would be if you couldn't count things, measure anything, do any calculations, or be precise about time, distance, or price. You wouldn't know how old you are, or how long you have to wait until vacation. We couldn't build anything accurately, we'd have no computers, no accurate recipes, no scores in games, or sports. You really wouldn't want to live without math!

Cookies

Ingredients:
Some flour
Some sugar
Some eggs
Some butter

Instructions:
Mix and bake in oven until done!

What Are Numbers?

Numbers give us a way of showing quantity—how many or how much, how long, and so on. Examples of numbers are "two," "thirty-five," and "six-hundred thousand." We write numbers down using the digits 0 to 9. A numeral is a set of digits used to write a number. So 2, 35, and 600,000 are all numerals. We use numbers for lots of different purposes. We use them to count, to carry out calculations, to measure things, and as labels. Numbers are also used in codes.

ARE NUMBERS REAL?
Philosophers argue about whether numbers and the rules of math are real, or just a human invention. Does it matter? What do you think?

A CASTAWAY ON a desert island might use numbers to count how long he or she has been marooned!

NUMBERS ARE GOOD for counting objects—but they don't give you any other information, such as size or quality. Is one big thing the same as one small thing? It is if you're just counting!

MEASURING. Some things—like volume, distance, and speed—can't be counted, so we have to measure them instead.

You Can Do It!

Try to spot all of the places you come across numbers in a day—from your alarm clock to the cereal box and bus schedule.

PHONE NUMBERS and car license plates use numbers to identify things—every phone or car has a different number.

WE CALCULATE WITH numbers in lots of areas of work, such as engineering, building, science, and art. These calculations are often used to keep us safe.

CODES AND LABELS. In a store, the bar code on anything you buy is a number. The number is a special code that tells the store what the item is.

BUYING AND SELLING. Prices and interest rates, special deals, and discounts are all part of the way we buy and sell things, and they all rely on numbers.

Does It Add Up?

When people first began to use numbers, they used them in tallies as a way to keep track of things. A tally matches things one-to-one, so one thing is used to represent another. Imagine you are a shepherd. You might use one pebble to represent one sheep. You need the same number of pebbles as sheep. If you drop a pebble into a pot for each sheep that passes, it's easy to see if you've got all your sheep. If there are pebbles left over, that means some of your flock are missing.

A TALLY IS more useful if you can count. If a tally doesn't match the number of the objects, and you can't count, then you won't know how many sheep are missing or how many to look for.

YOU CAN OFTEN see if one group is larger than another without having to count. Even some animals can do this, too. Lions will attack only a smaller pride, and they will run away from a larger pride.

FINGER-COUNTING is a bit like tallying, but you don't need any extra objects. Each finger is equivalent to an item; you could hold up five fingers to show you have five chickens.

Another sheep, another pebble...

If you are making a tally, draw vertical lines for the first four, then draw a bar across those lines for "5," then start again with more vertical lines.

NAME THAT NUMBER. Giving names to the numbers means you can count without using stones, sticks, fingers, or any other aid.

SOME BIRDS, as well as hyenas, chimpanzees, fish, and frogs, have a basic understanding of numbers. Birds can tell if any of their chicks are missing, for example.

HEAD TO TOE. If you used toes as well as fingers you could count to twenty. But the Oksapmin people of New Guinea do even better. Their body-counting system assigns numbers to 27 different parts of the body!

Where Did Numbers Come From?

Today, we use a place value system for writing numbers. This means the position of each digit tells us how much it is "worth." The digit on the right shows the units (ones), the next digit to the left shows the number of tens, the next digit to the left shows how many hundreds, and so on. So when we write "653," it really means (6x100)+(5x10)+(3x1). It's a very simple way of writing large numbers. But it's not the only method that has been used. Some older number systems were much harder to work with.

THE PLACE VALUE system means we can write really big numbers by just adding more and more digits.

THE NUMERALS 0 to 9 that we use today came originally from India, and were then used by Arab mathematicians in the Middle East and North Africa.

10

THE ROMANS USED LETTERS to build up numbers: I (for 1), V (5), X (10), L (50), C (100), and M (1,000). They repeated I, X, C, and M as necessary—so II = 2, III = 3, VII = 7 (5+2), XXXI = 31, and so on. To keep the numbers a bit shorter, they had another trick: IV = (5–1) =4, and IX = (10–1) =9. It could get rather complicated!

You Can Do It!

Try to write out the date of your birthday using Roman numerals in the form mm-dd-yyyy (month–day–year.)

LONG MULTIPLICATION. Imagine trying to do sums with Roman numerals—there's no easy way!

Why is this so hard?

PEOPLE IN EUROPE used Roman numerals until after 1200, when the mathematician Leonardo Fibonacci brought Arabic numerals to Italy. Arabic numerals didn't really become popular until the 1400s, even though they made math much easier.

No! One, not ten!

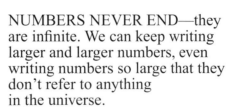

EARLY NUMBER SYSTEMS didn't use "zero" at the end of numbers. That made it hard to tell the difference between 4 and 40, or 6 and 600. Imagine how confusing that would be!

NUMBERS NEVER END—they are infinite. We can keep writing larger and larger numbers, even writing numbers so large that they don't refer to anything in the universe.

How Many Is 10?

We count using a base-10 number system. That means that we first count from 0 to 9, and then we start a new column for 10s (with a 1) and reuse the same digits to count higher (10, 11, 12...) When we get to 19, we increase the number in the 10s column (which becomes 2) and start again with 0 in the units column (20). We probably use base-10 because we have ten fingers. But it's not the only way to count. Any number can be used as a base.

A HUMAN ASTRONAUT and an alien that uses base-7 would not agree about how to write a number of objects. The astronaut would say there are 16 eggs, but in base-7 the alien would write this as 22 (2x7+2). There would still be just as many eggs, however it was written!

ANCIENT BABYLONIANS based their number system on 60. You can still see signs of this today: We divide a circle into 360 degrees (6x60) and an hour into 60 minutes.

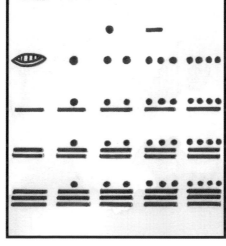

THE MAYANS used a system based on symbols for 1 and 5, and worked in base-20.

COMPUTERS OFTEN USE base-16, because this means they can store large numbers in less space. Letters are used as single digits for the number 10 (A) up to the number 15 (F).

AN ALIEN WITH seven tentacles might count in base-7 (see below). They would count 0 to 6, then start again, with 1 in the 7s column and 0 in the units column. So 10 would be 7, 11 would be 7+1=8, 12 would be 7+2=9, and so on. After 13, the alien would increase the 7s column to 2 and count 20!

What If You Can't Count?

Imagine you wanted to buy some rice. You wouldn't ask for 4,000 grains and wait for them to be counted, would you? It's much easier to measure the rice in some way, such as weighing it or measuring its volume. Or what if you wanted to buy orange juice for a picnic? You really can't count orange juice. When things can't be counted, we measure them instead. We measure anything that is continuous, like distance or liquids, and things that come as very small particles, like rice, sand, or flour. Many grocery items are also measured by weight, such as nuts and candy.

SAME MEASURES. It is important we all agree on the measures we use. A big bucket does not hold the same amount as a small bucket. If we all used different measures, we would argue all the time.

That's 113 feet.

No, it's 97 feet!

There are lots of different units of measurement. Some are a little strange. The heat of chili peppers is measured in Scoville heat units (named after American pharmacist Wilbur Scoville, who created this form of measurement).

WHOSE FOOT? Measures need to be consistent so that we can compare them with each other. If a foot is used as a measure of distance, we need to choose whose foot—otherwise we won't be able to agree on the distances we measure.

SOME MEASURES HAVE large and small versions. We measure the length of a bug in millimeters, but the distance to the Sun in millions of kilometers.

JOURNEY TIMES. How we measure things can change. Distances used to be measured in the time it took to travel, not the distance covered—it was a more useful thing to know.

Two days.

ONE SIZE FITS ALL. A person can't be in more than one place at a time. So to use someone's foot to measure things, we make a standard—a copy that stands in for the real foot, and is used by everybody.

How far to Rome?

15

Putting Math to Work

With numbers, we can do all kinds of calculations. Whenever we make anything, we measure and calculate distances, angles, areas, and volumes to make sure that things fit together properly and are strong, stable, and safe. Architects and engineers measure forces and stresses. It takes a lot of numbers to get complex systems like rockets, planes, and cars right. A tiny wrong calculation can mean the system doesn't work—and that could lead to disaster. Numbers are really important!

WE HAVE LIFTOFF! A space rocket launch involves a lot more numbers than just a countdown. Math is central to getting it right.

We have a total payload of 63,500 pounds (28,800 kg).

It will reach a maximum thrust of 1.2 million pounds (4,500 kilonewtons).

T + 20 seconds
Speed: 17,500 mph (28,000 kph)
Altitude: 650 feet (200 m) above sea level

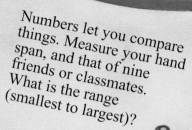

Numbers let you compare things. Measure your hand span, and that of nine friends or classmates. What is the range (smallest to largest)?

ONCE PEOPLE STARTED to own and fence in land, they needed to measure it. In ancient Egypt, the river Nile flooded every year. The Egyptians had to measure out their fields all over again after each flood.

THE I-35 BRIDGE over the Mississippi River collapsed in 2007 because it wasn't strong enough—the engineers had gotten the math wrong.

FORECASTING THE FUTURE. We count and measure things over time to make predictions. Knowing there are more storms helps us to measure climate change and plan for the future.

NUMBERS GIVE US the power to change things. By counting and comparing over time, we can figure out which animals are in danger and work to save them.

SAVE THE TIGER

IF WE MEASURE lots of examples of something, we can figure out what is normal and what to expect in the future. We can figure out averages—and spot things that are unusual.

Less Than Zero

Counting and measuring works when you have things to count or measure, but what happens when you don't? Negative numbers help you count things you don't have! If that sounds strange, think about what happens if you borrow something. Imagine you borrow an orange from a friend and eat it. You promise to give your friend an orange the next day. You now have less than no oranges, because as soon as you get one you have to give it away. You have minus one (-1) orange!

Brrrr! -20°F today!

SUBZERO. When numbers are used for a scale, they often go below zero. A thermometer shows negative numbers for very cold temperatures.

IF PEOPLE BORROW money to buy something, they have the thing, but they now have a negative amount of money, since they have to pay back what they borrowed.

You Can Do It!

How cold does it get in the winter where you live? Is it a negative number? Draw a chart to show what you will need to wear at different temperatures.

IF YOU KNOW you should have eight sheep but can only find five, add more sheep below zero on the number line until there are eight in total. You can see there are three still to find.

IN THE UNITED STATES, the ground floor is usually considered the first floor. But in some countries, the ground floor in a building is numbered zero because you don't have to go up or down to be on it. Below the ground floor, the floors have negative numbers because they are below zero.

GAME OVER. In some games, you can lose points by making a mistake. It's even possible to get a negative score if you're not very good at it, because you can lose more points than you win.

IS ZERO A NUMBER? If you have none of something, is that really a number? There are so many things you have none of—no pet elephants, no spaceships, no toy clowns . . .

19

Numbers, Codes, and Labels

Numbers can be used for more than counting, measuring, and calculating—although all those things are very useful. They can be used as labels or codes, too. When they are used in this way, they have nothing to do with math. Numbers are great for codes because you can keep adding more and more. Numbers used as codes and labels are all around us, from the channel numbers on the TV to the number on the door of your house or apartment.

COMPUTER CODE. Computers turn everything into a code made of numbers. So whether you're using the computer to write stories, look at videos, or edit your photos, it's all turned into numbers inside.

001001001
0011101001001
11000110110 0010
101001001110100
0011001001

Top Tip

To decide whether a number is used as a code, figure out whether you would do math with it. You wouldn't add up house numbers, would you?

15 + 17 = ?

PHONE NUMBERS ARE not entirely random numbers. They include codes that show the region where the phone is registered, or the network it uses.

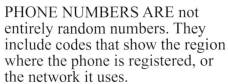

IN A CATALOG, every item has a code that identifies it. There might be bar codes to scan, too. A database stores all the information about an item under its number.

TV CHANNELS ARE identified by a number—but it's just a code. There is no real reason why a channel should have one number rather than another.

IDENTIFICATION. Lots of things are identified by numbers, from books to cars. Each item is given a special number—its own unique code. There's even a unique code on every book that identifies it to booksellers and libraries.

COLOR CODE. Sometimes numbers look like a code but are actually a kind of counting. RGB numbers tell a computer the amount of red, green, and blue needed to make up a particular color on the screen.

21

Do You Have the Time?

What time do you get up? What time does school end? How long are your classes? When's the next bus? How old are you? We measure and talk about time constantly, and we use numbers for it. Not just for hours of the day, but also for the date in the month, and the year. If we didn't have numbers it would be really difficult to keep track of time, or plan when to do things. Without numbers, it would be much harder to talk about what we've done during our day, or what we did in the past or hope to do in the future.

PRECISE TIMES MATTER. From catching the school bus to finishing your test in the time you're allowed, clocks help us keep track of when to do things, and when to stop doing things.

A YEAR IS the length of time it takes Earth to go around the Sun, and a day is the time it takes Earth to rotate. So there really are 365 days in a year—that's not a human invention!

You Can Do It!

On the weekend (not on a school day!) try living without looking at a clock or your watch all day. Eat when you're hungry and sleep when you're tired. Does it seem strange?

BUT NOT QUITE. There are actually 365.25 days in a year. It would be really inconvenient to start a new year partway through a day, so we have leap years to use up all the extra quarter days.

Happy New Year!

DEC

JAN 1

6:00AM

MATH AND TIME. Since we show times using numbers, we can also calculate with them. We can figure out durations (how long something takes) and intervals by adding and subtracting times.

SCHOOL TIMETABLE

	START	FINISH
MATH	9:00	9:45
Length of class: 45 mins		
HISTORY	10:00	10:45
Length of class: 45 mins		
PHYS. ED.	11:00	12:00
Length of class: 1 hour		

FAIRVIEW	BRISTOL	SPRINGFIELD
9:00	9:20	9:45
10:30	10:50	11:15
12:00	12:20	12:45
13:30	13:50	14:15

TIMETABLES USE NUMBERS to show the time when things start and finish, or when trains or buses get to different places. Without a timetable, you couldn't plan your trip.

HOW OLD? We count our age in years and use numbers to record dates. How would you know how old you were without numbers?

23

Precisely

Numbers give us a way of being precise. They help us figure out chances, probabilities, and proportions, making life less risky and unpredictable. They let us set limits and guidelines to keep ourselves and each other safe.

Lots of aspects of safety depend on using precise numbers: not too much and not too little of something. We make choices all the time depending on levels of risk and probabilities.

DOCTORS CALCULATE the doses of medicine needed for big people and small people. Too little won't make you better, and too much could be harmful. With the help of math, they can get it just right.

It will feel quite warm.

PRECISE NUMBERS ARE useful in lots of ways. What good would a weather forecast be without numbers to tell us the temperature?

NOT TOO FAST

SAFETY IN NUMBERS. Numbers let us set limits and guidelines to keep people safe. What if we had no speed limits, or no safety limits for electrical items? We could do something dangerous without knowing it.

WHAT ARE THE CHANCES? Probability is a measure of how likely something is to happen. If you had to pick one marble from a bag containing one black marble and four white ones, the chances of getting a black one would be one in five, or $\frac{1}{5}$.

Top Tip

Probability is just a guide: It doesn't tell us exactly what will happen. If there is an 85 percent chance of rain, it still might not rain.

IS IT WORTH IT? Probability helps us compare risks and benefits. You're more likely to enter a difficult race for a 10 percent chance of winning a bike than a 10 percent chance of winning a chocolate bar.

YOU CAN FIGURE OUT numbers from proportions. If you know half the children in a class of 30 like sandwiches, you need $\frac{1}{2} \times 30 = 15$ sandwiches. Without numbers, you'd end up with too many or too few—and possibly some unhappy kids!

A PROPORTION IS part of a whole group—it's a fraction. If an animal shelter had 90 dogs and 30 were brown, the proportion of brown dogs would be 30÷90, which is the same as $\frac{1}{3}$ (a third).

25

Numbers Don't Need Us

Whether or not we use numbers ourselves, the universe follows mathematical rules. Nature uses patterns, ratios, symmetry, and shapes that we describe using numbers and mathematics.

The rules of nature have always been there and will continue to be there forever, even if we stop using numbers or cease to exist.

The Fibonacci Sequence

NUMBERS IN NATURE. There are naturally occurring mathematic patterns in nature. One you can easily spot is the "golden spiral." It crops up in shells, plants, and fruit. If you trace the spines on a pineapple or the seeds in a sunflower head, you'll see they are packed into the same widening spiral pattern.

THE FIBONACCI SEQUENCE (right) is a special series of numbers that lies behind many patterns in nature, including the golden spiral. It was discovered by Fibonacci (see page 11). The number of petals on a flower is usually a Fibonacci number.

1, 2, 3, 5, 8, 13, 21, 34 ...

$$0+1=1$$
$$1+1=2$$
$$2+1=3$$
$$3+2=5$$

$$5+3=8$$
$$8+5=13$$
$$13+8=21$$
$$21+13=34 ...$$

THE FIBONACCI SEQUENCE is the series of numbers: 1, 2, 3, 5, 8, 13, 21, 34 . . . and so on. The next number is found by adding up the two numbers before it.

BEES PACK HONEY into hexagonal (six-sided) cells. It's the best shape for filling an area without gaps. Also, hexagons are extremely strong and don't bend out of shape under pressure.

You Can Do It!

Make your own symmetrical snowflake from paper. Fold a circle of paper in half and then into thirds, and cut a pattern into the sides. Open it up to see your snowflake.

THE MOVEMENT OF the planets is controlled by the gravity of the Sun and the other planets. They were all in the right places long before Newton figured out the laws of their movement in 1687.

NATURE LIKES SYMMETRY. Most animals have twofold symmetry like us. If you could fold yourself in half along the length of your spine, your right and left halves would match.

SPEEDING IN SPACE. The universe has a speed limit—nothing with mass can go faster than the speed of light: 186,282 miles a second (299,792 kilometers a second). A spaceship going that fast would take 4.2 years to get to the next nearest star.

SNOWFLAKES ARE SYMMETRICAL in a special way. They are made of a section repeated six times, rotating around the center.

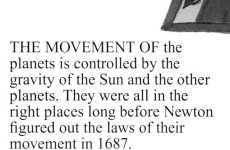

So, Would You Want to Live Without Math?

Numbers are everywhere in our lives, even places we can't see them or don't notice them. We are so used to them we rarely even think about how important they are. Numbers and calculations are essential to making and running the things we use every day. Without numbers used in mathematics, we couldn't make safe buildings or machines. We couldn't schedule our time, use money, have computers, or understand science. You really wouldn't want to live without math!

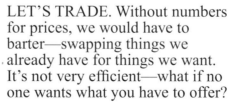

LET'S TRADE. Without numbers for prices, we would have to barter—swapping things we already have for things we want. It's not very efficient—what if no one wants what you have to offer?

IF WE COULDN'T measure time, it would be difficult to arrange anything. But people did manage to arrange to meet up before the invention of clocks!

IMAGINE ALL THE things we wouldn't have if we didn't have numbers. Numbers are vital in designing, making, testing, and running lots of things we take for granted.

You Can Do It!

You Can Do It!

Try going for a day—or even a few hours—without using numbers. Which things can't you do? How hard is it?

NUMBERS HELP TO keep us safe. Without them, we wouldn't be able to make anything accurately— things such as cars and buses might not work properly, and buildings might fall down.

IF WE EVER encounter aliens, they might have a completely different number system and way of doing math. Perhaps it's possible to express the same rules in different ways—but they would still be the same rules, however they are described.

Glossary

Architect Someone who designs structures such as buildings and bridges.

Babylonian A person who lived in the ancient city of Babylon, now in Iraq. The Babylonian civilization was destroyed about 3,500 years ago.

Database A collection of data (raw information) stored together on a computer in a way that means it can easily be searched or sorted into a different order.

Digit A single number character, 0 to 9.

Discount The amount by which a price is reduced in a special offer.

Engineer A person who designs machinery, structures, or equipment using a variety of materials.

Interest rate The rate at which extra money is charged when someone borrows a sum of money. The person pays back the original sum borrowed, plus an extra amount—perhaps 5 percent or 10 percent a year of the total they owe. The extra is called interest and is a charge for borrowing.

Interval The time that passes between two events.

Leap year A leap year is a year in which February is longer than it typically is in a non-leap-year year. In a leap year, February has 29 days instead of 28 days.

Mayan A person from the Maya culture in Central America. The Mayan number system was first used 3,000 years ago. The Mayan civilization was destroyed 500 years ago.

Negative number A number that is less than zero; it is shown by putting a minus sign (-) before the number.

Number line A line showing numbers, equally spaced, going up from zero toward the right (positive numbers) and down from zero toward the left (negative numbers). It can be used to help with calculations such as addition and subtraction.

Numeral A number written down using digits; 43, 891, and 5,139 are all examples of numerals.

Place value system A system of writing numbers that involves assigning value to a digit according to its place (position) in the number. In our place value system, the final digit (on the right) represents units (ones), the next to the left represents tens, the next hundreds, and so on.

Prediction A statement about what someone expects to happen, usually based on caclulations or other evidence.

Probability The likelihood that something will (or will not) happen, expressed as a decimal fraction between 0 and 1 or as a percentage.

Proportion A portion or fraction of a group, expressed as a fraction (a half, a quarter) or a percentage.

Symmetry The state of a shape being the same when folded, reflected, or rotated in one or more directions.

Tally A way of keeping score or count by using objects or making marks to correspond to the item or event being tracked—such as making a mark on the wall of a cave to record each day of being marooned on an island.

Index

A
age 23
alien 13, 29
angle 16
animals, counting 8, 9
architect 16
area 16
art 7
average 17

B
Babylonians 12
bar code 7, 21
base-10 12
bases 12
bees 27
body-counting 9
building 7
buying and selling 7

C
car license plates 7
chance 24
chili pepper 15
climate change 17
code 7, 20, 21
computer 12, 20, 21
counting 6

D
day 23
digit 6, 10
discount 7
distance 15, 16
duration 23

E
Egypt 17
engineering 7, 16

F
Fibonacci, Leonardo 11
Fibonacci sequence 26
finger-counting 8
foot 15
fraction 25

G
golden spiral 26
gravity 27

H
hexagon 27

I
I-35 bridge 17
infinity 11
interest rate 7
interval 23

M
Mayans 12
measuring 7, 14, 15, 16, 17
millimeter 15

N
negative number 18, 19
Newton, Isaac 27
number line 19
numeral 6, 10

P
phone number 7, 21
place value system 10
price 7, 28
probability 24, 25
proportion 24, 25

R
RGB number 21
Roman numerals 11

S
Scoville heat unit 15
snowflake 27
speed limit 24
symmetry 27

T
tally 8, 9
time 22, 28
timetable 23
trade 7

V
volume 14, 16

W
weather forecast 24
weight 14

Y
year 23

Z
zero 11, 18, 19

Amazing Number Facts

Infinite Infinities

There is no end to numbers—they go on forever. Infinity is the word we use to describe the numbers that go beyond what we are able to count. But there is more than one infinity. You could also count forever (to infinity) going *below* zero, which would be a negative infinity. And there are infinite decimal fractions between every pair of numbers. It's enough to make your brain spin.

Googol and Googolplex

The names for really large numbers, like billion and trillion, follow a rule that uses set prefixes (parts at the start of the word). But there are some special large numbers with their own names. A "googol" is 1 followed by 100 zeros (written 10^{100}). And a googolplex is 1 followed by a googol zeros (written 10^{googol}). The name "googol" was invented by nine-year-old Milton Sirotta in 1920. He was the nephew of mathematician Edward Kasner.

Sagan's Number

The number of stars in the observable universe is known as "Sagan's number," named after the astronomer Carl Sagan. The trouble is, we don't really know how many stars there are. When the number was first named it was thought to be around 10 sextillion (10^{22}). By 2010 it had risen to 300 sextillion—that's a lot more!

Amazing Sums

Some sums are fascinating:

$111111111 \times 111111111 = 12345678987654321$

and

$12+3-4+5+67+8+9=100$

Top Counting Aids

If you just count and calculate on your fingers, you can't get very far. Even adding toes doesn't help much. So people have used lots of different aids to help with counting.

Abacus An abacus is usually a wooden frame of rods threaded with beads. One row represents ones, the next tens, the next hundreds, and so on. Numbers are counted or calculated by moving beads in the different rows. Abacuses of various designs have been used for around 4,000 years.

Counting Board It's possible to make something like a simple abacus using just pebbles and dips in the sand or a board of wood. This is called a counting board. We don't know when they were first used, as dips in the sand don't last very long!

Quipu A quipu is a counting aid made of knotted strings. A main thick string has lots of thin strings looped over it, and then colored strings are knotted around the hanging strings, so it looks like a tangled fringe. It was used in South America by the Inca people, but we don't know exactly how they used it, since they had no written language.

Calculator The French mathematician Blaise Pascal made the first mechanical calculator in 1642, but the first one to be manufactured and sold appeared in 1851. The first electronic calculator was introduced in the 1960s. It's already impossible to imagine life without an electronic gadget to help us do math, whether it's a computer, calculator, or smartphone.